The Wafflehoffers Curious Maple

Fay B. Bolton

Illustrations By Gian Uy

Copyright © 2016 Fay B. Bolton

All rights reserved.

ISBN: 0692660011
ISBN-13: 978-0692660010

DEDICATION

To Charlotte and Katie -

Thank you for your support on this incredible journey.

To my mom, who without her these characters would never have been envisioned.

Chapter 1

"Hurry up, Maple. It's time to leave," shouted Mama Wafflehoffer as she washed the last plate from a breakfast of homemade waffles.

"Coming!" yelled Maple as she ran outside and climbed into the car. She was curious as to what animals she would meet, on Uncle Pete's farm.

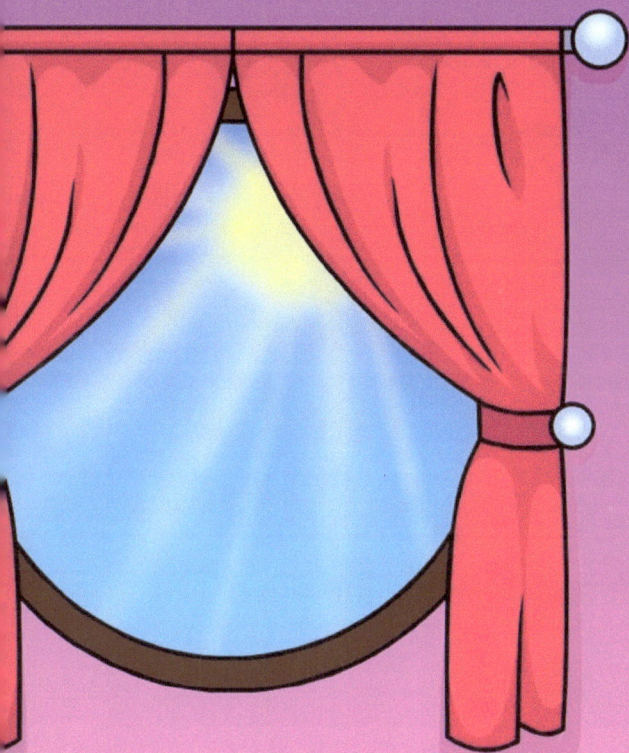

Chapter 2

"Welcome," announced Uncle Pete as he greeted everyone in the farmyard. "It's lovely to see you all again. I hope the drive didn't take too long?"

"It took forever," huffed Maple.

"Oh! Sorry to hear that. Well, Aunt Martha is inside preparing lunch. I hope everyone is hungry."

Wafflehoffers were *always* hungry.

Maple took a deep breath when she entered the kitchen. The smell of Aunt Martha's waffles filled her nostrils. Her stomach growled.

Aunt Martha's waffles were the best in all of Waffleville. She'd won first place for five years in a row at the County Fair.

Maple took her seat at the kitchen table. "It smells delicious!"

"Why thank you, Maple. Help yourself," said Aunt Martha. "What's the matter, Zack? Not hungry?"

Maple's brother Zack lowered his head. He was tired of always eating waffles.

During lunch, Uncle Pete shared stories about the farm. A new foal had been born! Maple couldn't wait to meet it. She'd never seen a baby horse before.

"OK, kids, it's time to go outside and play. Mind you don't go near the mare and her foal," warned Uncle Pete.

Chapter 3

"Where are you headed?" asked Zack when they got outside.

"I'm going to look for the foal," said Maple.

"Don't you dare. Uncle Pete told us to stay away," warned Zack as he headed into the barn.

When Maple heard the word "dare," she smiled and felt more committed than ever to find the foal.

The sun's rays warmed Maple's face and she sang a happy song as she walked down the dirt path, followed by Butter, the family dog.

"Oh! Where, oh where can that little foal be? Is he hiding behind the big stone wall or a big oak tree?"

Maple soon came upon a black cat.

"Excuse me, Mr. Cat, but have you seen a foal?"

"A foal, you say? If I'm correct from what I can recall, it has four long legs with hooves for feet and can gallop as fast as the wind does blow."

"Yes it does!" responded Maple.

"I wish I could help you, but the farmer wants me to stay here and chase away any pesky mice that try to eat his grain," said the cat.

Maple thanked the cat then continued down the path as she sang her happy song. "Oh! Where, oh where can that little foal be? Is he hiding behind the big stone wall or a big oak tree?"

The next animal Maple came upon was a cow.

"Hello, Mrs. Cow. I was wondering if you'd seen a foal?"

"A foal, you say? If I'm correct from what I can recall, it has two pointed ears, on the top of its head, that listened for danger before it fled."

"Yes it does," responded Maple.

"I wish I could help you, but the farmer keeps me in this field all day, eating grass so I can produce milk for them to drink. Maybe you should ask the farmer's dog," suggested the cow. "You'll find him guarding the sheep."

Maple thanked the cow then continued down the path as she sang her happy song. "Oh! Where, oh where can that little foal be? Is he hiding behind the big stone wall or a big oak tree?"

Maple soon came upon a herd of sheep grazing in the field.

"Excuse me, but does anyone know where I can find the farmer's dog?"

"Here I am," responded a black-and-white sheepdog. "I hear you're looking for a foal. Does it have two big nostrils at the end of its nose so it can smell flowers wherever it goes?"

"Yes it does," responded Maple.

"Follow the path through the dense trees to the far end of the farmer's land. You will find the mare and her foal grazing in a field. Mind you don't go near them," instructed the farmer's dog.

"Can you show me the way?"

"Sorry, my job is to stay here and keep a watchful eye on the sheep. I don't want a wolf eating them for its supper."

Maple thanked the farmer's dog and continued on her way.

The path ahead was dark and scary. Tall trees cast long shadows on the ground.

The air felt damp and smelled musty.

"Oh! Where, oh where can that little foal be? Is he hiding behind the big stone wall or a big oak tree?" she mumbled to herself as she sprinted down the path.

I hope there are no wolves, she thought.

Chapter 4

Maple reached a clearing and saw the mare and her foal lying down in a field.

"Stay here," Maple ordered Butter before she climbed over the stone wall and tiptoed closer to the horses. She cautiously took one step, then another and was taken by complete surprise when the mare sprang to her feet and galloped towards Maple.

Maple's heart thumped loud as she ran towards the wall, hoping to escape. But the mare was too fast for Maple and began running circles around her.

"HELP!" shouted Maple at the top of her lungs. She closed her eyes and wished that she could be transported back to the safety of her parents.

"Mom, stop scaring the little girl," said the gentle voice of the foal.

"Were you scared?" asked the mare.

"A little," responded Maple, shaking.

"What are you doing here?" asked the mare. "Weren't you warned to stay away?"

"I was, but I wanted to see your foal. May I ask why I was told to stay away from you?" inquired Maple.

"Because of an accident," explained the mare. "You see, your uncle came into my field, and when he got up close my foal bit me. I was so startled that I accidentally kicked your uncle."

"Now I understand," responded Maple.

"It was all a terrible accident. The problem now is that your uncle has banished us to this field because he thinks I'm dangerous. We're awfully sad and lonely and all we want is to get back to our friends."

Chapter 5

"I have an idea!" announced Maple. "May I put this halter on you?"

"Of course," said the mare.

Maple buckled the halter securely while explaining her plan to the mare.

"It all sounds good," responded the mare. "But I don't think your uncle will believe you."

"Then we'll just have to make him believe!" exclaimed Maple.

She marched the mare and her foal through the pasture gate, and up the path. Butter, the dog, happily pranced behind, keeping a safe distance.

At first, as they walked up the path, all the farm animals watched in disbelief. But soon their captivated silence turned into loud cheers!

Maple's family came outside into the farmyard to see what the

commotion was all about.

Chapter 6

Maple walked toward her family and Uncle Pete.

Before anyone could say a word, she blurted out in a single breath: "Uncle Pete, it was all an accident! The mare didn't mean to kick you. It was a huge mistake and she's terribly sorry for what she did. Can you please forgive her?"

"Didn't I tell you how dangerous she was?" asked Uncle Pete flaring his nostrils.

"You told me to stay away, but you never explained why," replied Maple.

The silent pause was interrupted by the sound of giggling, and then roars of laughter filled the air. The mare had risen up her head for all to see, curling her upper lip and exposing her teeth in an attempt to smile.

"Well, I'll be. You're not dangerous after all. You let Maple lead you down the path without trying to run away," declared Uncle Pete.

"Let's forget about what happened."

"Neigh!" responded the mare. Then she winked at Maple.

Mama Wafflehoffer gave Maple a big hug. "You truly are my brave little girl."

Chapter 7

"Maple, I want you to follow me into the barn," said Uncle Pete. "I should have told you that the mare had kicked me and that's why I wanted you to stay away. I just didn't want you to get hurt."

Maple felt guilty. If the mare were truly dangerous, she could have gotten hurt.

Uncle Pete could tell that Maple had learned her lesson.

"OK, Maple, you did still disobey me, so here is the bucket of brushes. And look, here's a friendly horse for you to start grooming!

Maple picked up a brush and began grooming the mare. The foal stepped forward and nuzzled his head playfully on Maple's arm. Maple smiled.

Chapter 8

After Maple was finished with her chores, the Wafflehoffers headed home.

That night for dinner, Mama Wafflehoffer baked Maple her favorite, blueberry waffles.

Chapter 9

Then Maple fell asleep, dreaming about her wonderful day on the farm. She hoped that they'd visit Uncle Pete again soon.

THE END

www.ingramcontent.com/pod-product-compliance
Lightning Source LLC
LaVergne TN
LVHW072052070426
835508LV00002B/53